Langenscheidt

Japanese
at your Fingertips

Tien Tammada

Langenscheidt

Forword

Traveling to foreign or distant lands is a wonderful and exciting thing to do. In fact, it probably features top of the list in worldwide rankings.

However, before every journey to a foreign country, there is a hurdle to be cleared and this hurdle is called "foreign language". For many, this hurdle seems insurmountable. As a result, they have to give up their life's dream.

What a pity!

You may be planning a week's holiday in Japan to experience the magical countryside or considering moving to live and work in Japan.

Whatever your motivation, don't wait.
Don't let this hurdle stop you from fulfilling your lifelong dream!
Have the courage to embark on this exciting journey to the Japanese language – **now**!

Once you've made the decision, you'll find that this book provides you with the first helpful steps. You don't need to book a language course and you don't need to worry about complicated grammatical points. To make it easy for you, we have introduced a unique color system to help you match the Romaji (Latin transcription) to the Japanese characters. The meaning of the colors is explained on the last page.

Anyone who has mastered a foreign language knows that the essential and really crucial thing about learning a language is actually quite simple: you need to jump in at the deep end. Once you're in the water, everything flows from there.

Jump and don't think twice! You'll learn by doing, not by preparing. The pictures, the selection of important words and useful phrases that you'll find in this book are an important first step. As soon as you come up against the first language hurdle, you can open the book to the appropriate page and find the necessary words and phrases.

If that doesn't work, try pointing to the relevant picture or sentence with your finger. People will know immediately what you mean.
It's really all very easy and convenient. That's why the book is called "Japanese at your Fingertips".

Content

Useful daily conversations

にちじょうかいわ
日常会話
nichijō kaiwa

Greetings

あいさつ
挨拶
aisatsu

おはようございます。	こんにちは。	こんばんは。
ohayō gozaimasu	konnichiwa	konbanwa
Good morning!	Good afternoon!	Good evening!

<ruby>お元気<rt>げんき</rt></ruby>ですか。

ogenki desuka

How are you?

<ruby>元気<rt>げんき</rt></ruby>です。

genki desu*

I'm fine, thank you.

* In the word "desu", u is silent.

はい ｜ いいえ

はい	いいえ
hai	iie
Yes.	No.

ありがとう。	ありがとう ございます。	どういたしまして。
arigatō	arigatō gozaimasu	dōitashimashite
Thanks.	Thank you very much.	You're welcome.

私の名前は...です。 watashino namaewa... desu	My name is...
お名前は何ですか。 onamaewa nandesuka	What is your name?
はじめまして。 hajimemashite	Nice to meet you.
アメリカから来ました amerikakara kimashita	I'm from America.
日本語を話せません。 nihongoo hanasemasen	I cannot speak Japanese.
少し日本語を話せます。 sukoshi nihongoo hanasemasu	I can speak a little Japanese.
日本語で何と言いますか。 nihongode nanto iimasuka	How do you say that in Japanese?
もう1回言って頂けますか。 mōikkai itte itadakemasuka	Could you say that again, please?
ゆっくり話して頂けますか。 yukkuri hanashite itadakemasuka	Could you speak more slowly, please?

すみません、...へは
どうやって行きますか。

sumimasen, ...ewa **dōyatte** ikimasuka

Excuse me, how do I get to ...?

どういう意味ですか。 dōiu imi desuka	What does that mean?
それは何ですか。 sorewa nandesuka	What is that?
何と言いましたか。 nanto iimashitaka	I beg your pardon? (What did you say?)
すみません。 sumimasen	Excuse me.
大丈夫です。 daijōbudesu	No problem.
ここはどこですか。 kokowa dokodesuka	Where am I?
...へはどうやって行きますか。 ...ewa dōyatte ikimasuka	How do I get to ...?
ここからどれ位の距離ですか。 kokokara dorekurainokyori desuka	How far is it from here?

... さん ... san	Mr.
... さん ... san	Miss. , Mrs.
... ちゃん / ... くん ... chan / ... kun	suffix often added to child's name (...chan for girl or boy/...kun for boy)
... はどこですか。 ... wa dokodesuka	Where is ...?
これをお願いします。 koreo onegaishimasu	This one, please.
いくらですか。 ikura desuka	How much does it cost?
これが好きです。 korega sukidesu	I like this.
それが嫌いです。 sorega kiraidesu	I don't like that.
まあまあ māmā	So-so.
すごい！ sugōi	Awesome!

<ruby>素<rt>す</rt></ruby><ruby>晴<rt>ば</rt></ruby>らしい！ subarashii	Wonderful!
<ruby>最<rt>さい</rt></ruby><ruby>高<rt>こう</rt></ruby>！ saikō	Great!
<ruby>良<rt>よ</rt></ruby>い／いい yoi / ii	good
とてもいい totemo ii	very good
<ruby>悪<rt>わる</rt></ruby>い warui	bad
ひどい hidoi	terrible, awful
たくさん takusan	a lot of
<ruby>少<rt>すこ</rt></ruby>し sukoshi	little, few
いくつか ikutsuka	some
ちょっと<ruby>待<rt>ま</rt></ruby>ってください。 chottomatte kudasai	Wait a moment, please.
<ruby>少<rt></rt></ruby>々お<ruby>待<rt>ま</rt></ruby>ちください。 shōshō omachi kudasai	One moment, please. (honorific)

近いうちに会いましょう！ chikaiuchini aimashō	See you soon!
また会いましょう！ mata aimashō	See you again!
また明日！ mata ashita	See you tomorrow!
さようなら！ sayōnara	Good bye!
誰？ dare	Who?
何？ nani	What?
どこ？ doko	Where?
いつ？ itsu	When?
なぜ？/ どうして？ naze / dōshite	Why?
どうやって？ dōyatte	How?
いくら？ / いくつ？ ikura / ikutsu	How much? / How many?

いってきます!
ittekimasu

Good bye! / I'm off! (and I will come back again.)

いってらっしゃい！
itterasshai

Good bye! (go and come back safely)

At the airport

<ruby>空港<rt>くうこう</rt></ruby>にて kūkō nite

<ruby>空港<rt>くうこう</rt></ruby>

kūkō

the airport

<ruby>入国審査<rt>にゅうこくしんさ</rt></ruby> は どこですか。

nyūkoku-shinsawa dokodesuka

Where is passport control?

<ruby>飛行機<rt>ひ こう き</rt></ruby> hikōki

すみません、<ruby>市内<rt>しない</rt></ruby>へはどうやって<ruby>行<rt>い</rt></ruby>きますか。

sumimasen, shinaiewa dōyatte ikimasuka

Excuse me, how can I get to the city?

<ruby>駅<rt>えき</rt></ruby>はどこですか。

ekiwa dokodesuka

Where is the train station?

すみません、

<ruby>出口<rt>でぐち</rt></ruby>はどこですか。

sumimasen,
deguchiwa dokodesuka

Excuse me, where is the exit?

the airplane

<ruby>バス停<rt>てい</rt></ruby>はどこですか。
basuteiwa dokodesuka

Where is the bus stop?

タクシー<ruby>乗場<rt>のりば</rt></ruby>はどこですか。
takushī-noribawa dokodesuka

Where is the taxi stand?

かんこう あんないじょ
観光案内所 はどこですか。
kanko-annaijowa dokodesuka
Where is tourist information?

てごろ　　　　　　おし
手頃なホテルを教えてもらえますか。
tegorona hoteruo oshiete moraemasuka
Can you recommend an affordable hotel?

ちゅうしんがい
中心街までどれくらいですか。
chūshingaimade dorekuraidesuka
How far is it to downtown?

お　　　　ばしょ　　おし
降りる場所を教えてください。
oriru bashoo oshiete kudasai
Could you tell me when to get off please?

バス

basu

bus

この<ruby>住所<rt>じゅうしょ</rt></ruby> まで<ruby>送<rt>おく</rt></ruby>ってください。
konojūshomade okutte kudasai
Drive me to this address, please.

(<ruby>乗車料金<rt>じょうしゃ りょうきん</rt></ruby> は) いくらですか。
(jōsha-ryōkinwa) ikuradesuka
How much does the ride cost?

クレジットカードで<ruby>払<rt>はら</rt></ruby>えますか。
kurejittokādode haraemasuka
Can I pay by credit card?

ありがとうございました。
arigatō gozaimashita
Thank you very much.

タクシー
takushī

taxi

でんしゃ

電車

densha

train

ち か て つ

地下鉄

chikatetsu

subway

ろ めん でんしゃ

路面電車

romendensha

tram

しんかんせん
新幹線
shinkansen

HST (High Speed Train)

ふね
船
fune

ship

Accommodation

しゅくはくしせつ
宿泊施設
shukuhaku shisetsu

くうしつ
空室はありますか。 — Is there any room available?
kūshitsuwa arimasuka

へや み
部屋を見せてください。 — May I see the room, please?
heyao misete kudasai

いくらですか。 — How much is it?
ikura desuka

ちょうしょくつ
朝食付きですか。 — Is breakfast included?
chōshoku-tsuki desuka

なまえ よやく
...の名前で予約しました。 — I have booked (a room)
...nonamaede yoyaku in the name of ...
shimashita

これが私<ruby>私<rt>わたし</rt></ruby>のパスポートです。　Here is my passport.
korega watashinopasupōto desu

インターネットはありますか。　Do you have wireless Intenet?
intānettowa arimasuka

<ruby>金庫<rt>きんこ</rt></ruby>はありますか。　Do you have a safe?
kinkowa arimasuka

チェックアウトは<ruby>何時<rt>なんじ</rt></ruby>ですか。　When do I have to check out?
chekku-autowa nanji desuka

<ruby>受付<rt>うけつけ</rt></ruby>はいつも<ruby>開<rt>あ</rt></ruby>いていますか。　Is reception open all the time?
uketsukewa itsumo aiteimasuka

...部屋をお願いします。

...beyao onegaishimasu

I would like a room for (one person).

1人
hitori

one person.

2人
futari

two people.

かぞく
家族
kazoku
a family.

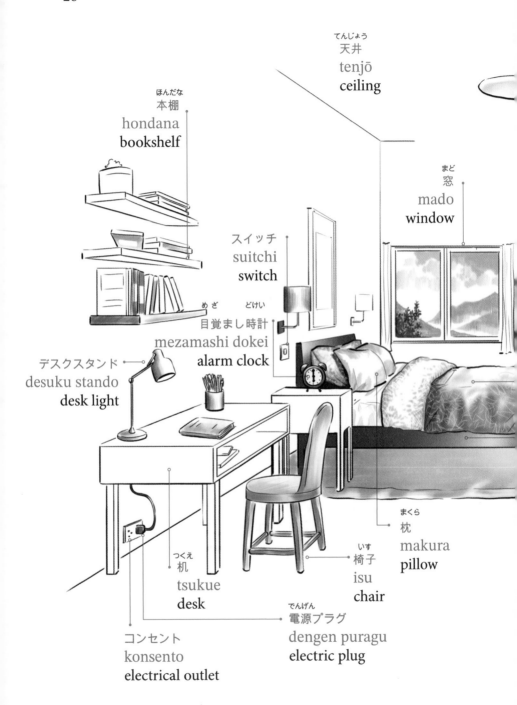

てんじょう
天井
tenjō
ceiling

ほんだな
本棚
hondana
bookshelf

まど
窓
mado
window

スイッチ
suitchi
switch

めざ　　どけい
目覚まし時計
mezamashi dokei
alarm clock

デスクスタンド
desuku stando
desk light

まくら
枕
makura
pillow

つくえ
机
tsukue
desk

いす
椅子
isu
chair

でんげん
電源プラグ
dengen puragu
electric plug

コンセント
konsento
electrical outlet

エアコン
eakon
air conditioner

カーテン
kāten
curtain

ハンガー
hangā
clothes hanger

ひ だ
引き出し
hikidashi
drawer

ぼうし
帽子
bōshi
hat

かばん
kaban
handbag

Tシャツ
T-shatsu
T-shirts

ズボン
zubon
pants

くつ
靴
kutsu
shoes

もうふ
毛布
mōfu
blanket

じゅうたん
絨毯
jyūtan
carpet

ベット
betto
bed

In the bedroom
しんしつ
寝室 shinshitsu

In the bathroom

浴室 yokushitsu
<small>よくしつ</small>

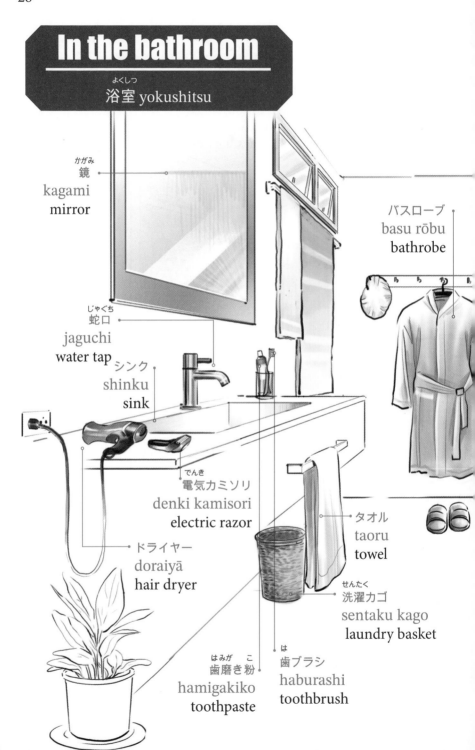

かがみ
鏡
kagami
mirror

じゃぐち
蛇口
jaguchi
water tap

シンク
shinku
sink

バスローブ
basu rōbu
bathrobe

でんき
電気カミソリ
denki kamisori
electric razor

ドライヤー
doraiyā
hair dryer

タオル
taoru
towel

せんたく
洗濯カゴ
sentaku kago
laundry basket

はみが　こ
歯磨き粉
hamigakiko
toothpaste

は
歯ブラシ
haburashi
toothbrush

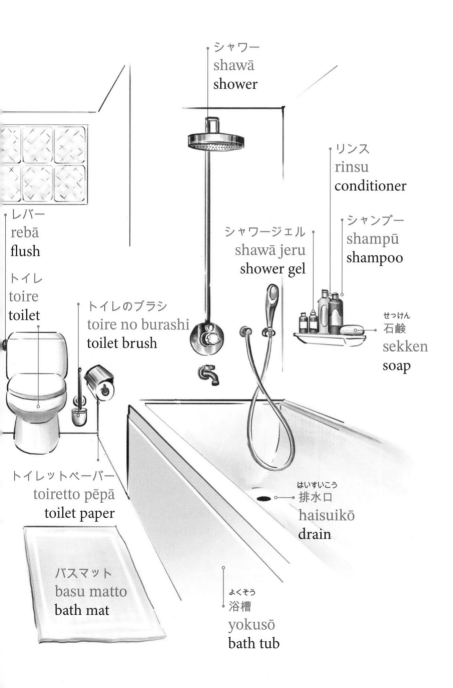

シャワー
shawā
shower

リンス
rinsu
conditioner

レバー
rebā
flush

シャンプー
shampū
shampoo

シャワージェル
shawā jeru
shower gel

トイレ
toire
toilet

せっけん
石鹸
sekken
soap

トイレのブラシ
toire no burashi
toilet brush

トイレットペーパー
toiretto pēpā
toilet paper

はいすいこう
排水口
haisuikō
drain

バスマット
basu matto
bath mat

よくそう
浴槽
yokusō
bath tub

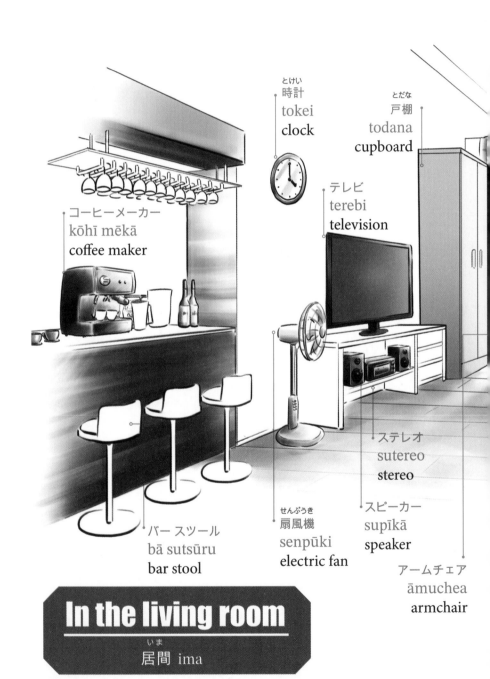

とけい
時計
tokei
clock

とだな
戸棚
todana
cupboard

テレビ
terebi
television

コーヒーメーカー
kōhī mēkā
coffee maker

ステレオ
sutereo
stereo

バー スツール
bā sutsūru
bar stool

せんぷうき
扇風機
senpūki
electric fan

スピーカー
supīkā
speaker

アームチェア
āmuchea
armchair

In the living room
いま
居間 ima

シャンデリア
shanderia
chandelier

ピアノ
piano
piano

え
絵
e
picture

ほん
本
hon
book

バイオリン
baiorin
violin

テーブル
tēburu
table

かびん
花瓶
kabin
vase

はな
花
hana
flowers

リモコン
rimokon
remote control

ソファー
sofā
sofa

でんわ
電話
denwa
telephone

コップ
koppu
glass

カップ
kappu
cup

フライパン
furaipan
frying pan

びん
瓶
bin
bottle

ワイングラス
wain gurasu
wine glass

はし
(お)箸
(o)hashi
chopsticks

さら
皿
sara
plate

あわだ き
泡立て器
awadateki
whisk

スプーン
supūn
spoon

フォーク
fōku
fork

いた
まな板
manaita
chopping board

じゃぐち
蛇口
jaguchi
tap

でんし
電子レンジ
denshi renji
microwave

33

In the kitchen

だいどころ
台所 daidokoro

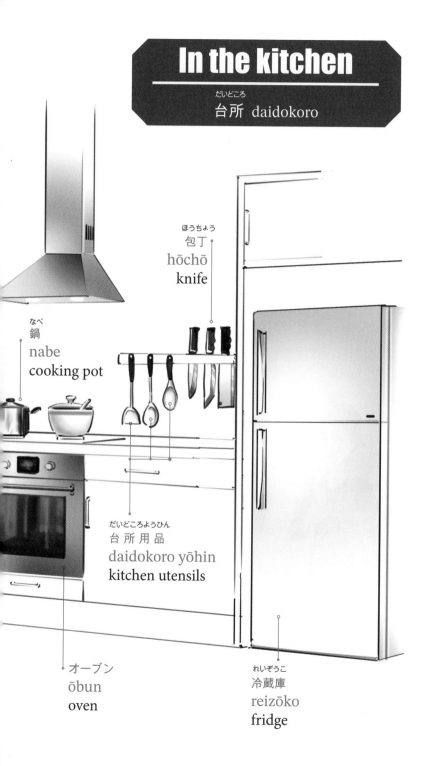

ほうちょう
包丁
hōchō
knife

なべ
鍋
nabe
cooking pot

だいどころようひん
台所用品
daidokoro yōhin
kitchen utensils

オーブン
ōbun
oven

れいぞうこ
冷蔵庫
reizōko
fridge

Excursions (in the city and in the countryside)

りょこう　としん　こうがい
旅行 (都心と郊外)
ryokō (toshin to kōgai)

へん　　かんこう　めいしょ
この辺に観光名所はありますか。
konohenni kankō-meshowa arimasuka

Are there any tourist attractions in this area?

でんとうてき　　きょうど　りょうり　　　　　あじ
伝統的な郷土料理はどこで**味わえます**か。
dentōtekina kyōdo-ryōriwa dokode ajiwaemasuka

Where can I try traditional local foods?

Excursions by train

電車での旅行 densha deno ryokō

駅はどこですか。
ekiwa dokodesuka

Where is the train station?

券売機はどこですか。
kenbaikiwa dokodesuka

Where is the ticket vending machine?

切符売り場はどこですか。
kippu-uribawa dokodesuka

Where is the ticket office?

切符はいくらですか。
kippuwa ikuradesuka

How much does the ticket cost?

指定席を 1 枚お願いします。
shitei-sekio ichi-mai onegaishimasu

One reserved seat ticket, please.

自由席を1枚お願いします。
jiyū-sekio ichi-mai onegaishimasu

One unreserved seat ticket, please.

片道切符を 1 枚ください。
katamichikippuo ichi-mai kudasai

A one-way ticket, please.

おうふく きっぷ　　　ねが
往復切符をお願いします。
ōfuku kippuo onegaishimasu

A round-trip ticket, please.

していせき　　　よやく
指定席を予約したいです。
shitei-sekio yoyakushitaidesu

I would like to book a reserved seat.

でんしゃ　　なんじ　で
電車は何時に出ますか。
denshawa nanjini demasuka

What time does the train leave?

の　　か
乗り換えは ありますか。
norikaewa arimasuka

Do I have to change trains?

つぎ　えき
次の駅はどこですか。
tsugino ekiwa dokodesuka

What is the next station?

お　　えき　おし
降りる駅で教えてください。
oriru ekide oshiete kudasai

Please tell me when I have to get off.

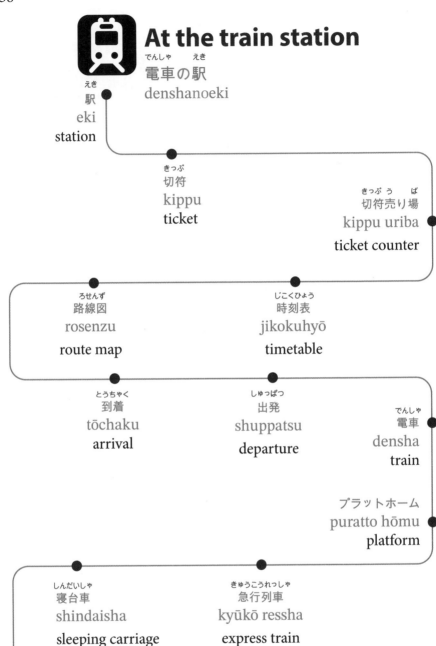

At the train station

でんしゃ えき
電車の駅
denshanoeki

えき
駅
eki
station

きっぷ
切符
kippu
ticket

きっぷ う ば
切符売り場
kippu uriba
ticket counter

ろせんず
路線図
rosenzu
route map

じこくひょう
時刻表
jikokuhyō
timetable

とうちゃく
到着
tōchaku
arrival

しゅっぱつ
出発
shuppatsu
departure

でんしゃ
電車
densha
train

プラットホーム
puratto hōmu
platform

しんだいしゃ
寝台車
shindaisha
sleeping carriage

きゅうこうれっしゃ
急行列車
kyūkō ressha
express train

していせき
指定席
shiteiseki
reserved-seat

じゆうせき
自由席
jiyūseki
unreserved-seat

せき　よやく
席の予約
sekinoyoyaku
seat reservation

かたみち
片道
katamichi
one-way

おうふく
往復
ōfuku
round-trip

ついかりょうきん
追加料金
tsuika-ryōkin
surcharge

じょうしゃ
乗車
jōsha
getting on a train

げしゃ
下車
gesha
getting off a train

の　　か
乗り換え
norikae
changing trains

なんじ でんしゃ ちかてつ
何時に電車 / バス / 地下鉄 /

ろめんでんしゃ しゅっぱつ
路面電車は 出発しますか。

nanjini densha/basu/chikatetsu/
romen denshawa shuppatsushimasuka

What time does the train / the bus /
the subway / the tram / leave?

すみません、切符（きっぷ）を買（か）うのを

手伝（てつだ）ってもらえますか。

sumimasen, kippuokaunoo tetsudatte
moraemasuka

Excuse me, can you help me to buy a ticket please?

...へ行（い）きたいです。

... e ikitaidesu

I want to go to ....

Excursions by bus and tram

バスと<ruby>路面電車<rt>ろめんでんしゃ</rt></ruby>での<ruby>観光<rt>かんこう</rt></ruby> basuto romendenshadeno kankō

バス basu	bus
<ruby>バス停<rt>てい</rt></ruby> basutei	bus stop
<ruby>路面電車<rt>ろめんでんしゃ</rt></ruby> romendensha	tram

<ruby>路面電車<rt>ろ めん でん しゃ</rt></ruby>の<ruby>停留所<rt>ていりゅうじょ</rt></ruby>は**どこですか**。
romendenshano teiryūjowa **dokodesuka**
Where is the tram stop?

<ruby>路面電車<rt>ろめんでんしゃ</rt></ruby>の<ruby>停留所<rt>ていりゅうじょ</rt></ruby> romendenshano teiryūjo	tram stop
<ruby>整理券<rt>せいりけん</rt></ruby> seiriken	numbered ticket
<ruby>バス運賃<rt>うんちん</rt></ruby> basu unchin	bus fare
<ruby>降車<rt>こうしゃ</rt></ruby>ボタン kōshabotan	stop button (on a bus)
<ruby>バス運転手<rt>うんてんしゅ</rt></ruby> basu untenshu	bus driver

…はどこですか。

…wa dokodesuka

Where is…?

バス停はどこですか。
てい

basuteiwa dokodesuka

Where is the bus stop?

しんごうき
信号機
shingōki
traffic lights

オートバイ
ōtobai
motorcycle

じてんしゃ
自転車
jitensha
bicycle

くるま
車
kuruma

car

Travelling on your own by car, motocycle, bicycle and on foot

車、オートバイ、自転車、徒歩での移動
kuruma, ōtobai, jitensha, toho deno idō

通り tōri	street
交差点 kōsaten	intersection
まっすぐ行く / 直進する massugu iku / chokushinsuru	go straight on
右に曲がる / 右折する migini magaru/ usetsusuru	turn right
左に曲がる / 左折する hidarini magaru/ sasetsusuru	turn left
ガソリンスタンドはどこですか。 gasorin sutandowa dokodesuka	Where is the gas station?
ここ koko	here
あそこ asoko	over there
近い chikai	near
遠い tōi	far
保険 hoken	insurance
どのガソリンを入れたらいいですか。 donogasorino iretara iidesuka	What kind of gas should I put in?

Art and leisure time activities

アートとレジャー活動 atoto rejia katusdō

歌舞伎
kabuki
classical Japanese
dance-drama

相撲
sumō
sumo

映画館
eigakan
movie theater

アートギャラリー
āto gyararī
art gallery

美術館 / 博物館
bijutsukan / hakubutsukan
art museum / museum

プール
pūru
swimming pool

おんせん
温泉
onsen
hot spring

サウナ
sauna
sauna

こうえん
公園
kōen
park

ジム
jimu
gym

Tourist attractions

かんこうめいしょ
観光名所 kankō meisho

とうきょう　　　　　とうきょう
東京タワー　（東京）
tokyo tawā (Tokyo)

ふじさん　　しずおか　　やまなし
富士山　（静岡 /　山梨）
Mt. Fuji (Shizuoka/Yamanashi)

こうとくいん　だいぶつ　　かながわ
高徳院 の大仏 (神奈川)
kōtoku-innodaibutsu
(Kanagawa)

ひめじじょう　　ひょうご
姫路城 (兵庫)
himeji-jo (Hyogo)

ひろしま へいわ　きねんひ　　（ ひろしま ）
広 島 平 和 記 念 碑　　（ 広 島 ）
hiroshima heiwa kinenhi
(Hiroshima)

きよみずでら　　　（ きょうと ）
清 水 寺　　　（ 京 都 ）
kiyomizu-dera
(Kyoto)

ちゅうぶさんがくこくりつこうえん
中 部 山 岳 国 立 公 園
chubu Sangaku kokuritsu koen
Chubu Sangaku National Park
(Nagano, Gifu, Toyama, Niigata)

きんかくじ　（ きょうと ）
金 閣 寺　（ 京 都 ）
kinkaku-ji (Kyoto)

Tourist attractions

<ruby>観光名所<rt>かんこうめいしょ</rt></ruby> Kankō meisho

かんこうめいしょ
観光名所 Kankō meisho

いつくしま　　（ひろしま）
厳 島 　　（広 島 ）
Itsukushima (Hiroshima)

こうきょ　（とうきょう）
皇居 （東京 ）
Kōkyo (Tokyo)

おおさかじょう（おおさか）
大 阪 城 （大 阪 ）
Osaka-jō (Osaka)

とうだいじ （なら）
東大寺 （奈良 ）
Todai-ji (Nara)

白川郷　（岐阜）
Shirakawago (Gifu)

富良野　（北海道）
Furano (Hokkaido)

At the bakery

パン屋
panya

あんぱん
anpan

bread filled with red bean paste

クリームパン
kurīmu pan

cream bread

ツナパン
tuna pan

tuna bread

カレーパン
karē pan

curry bread

メロンパン
meron pan

melon bread

パン
pan

---

bread

<ruby>焼<rt>や</rt></ruby>きそばパン
yakisoba pan

---

yakisoba bread

<ruby>明太子<rt>めんたいこ</rt></ruby>パン
mentaiko pan

---

mentaiko bread

ラム肉
ramu niku
lamb meat

子羊
koshistuji
lamb

At the butchers

にくや
肉屋 nikuya

うし
牛
ushi
cow

ぎゅうにく
牛肉
gyū niku
beef

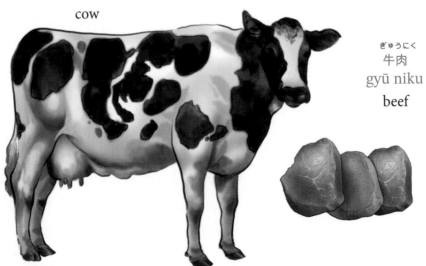

いのしし
猪
inoshishi
boar

かも
鴨
kamo
duck

かもにく
鴨肉
kamo niku
duck meat

いのししにく
猪肉
inoshishi niku
boar meat

ぶた
豚
buta
pig

ぶたにく
豚肉
buta niku
pork

とり
鶏
tori
chicken

とりにく
鶏肉
tori niku
chicken meat

At the fishmonger

<ruby>魚屋<rt>さかなや</rt></ruby> sakanaya

ぶり
buri
yellowtail

えび
ebi

shrimp

うなぎ
unagi
eel

<ruby>伊勢えび<rt>いせ</rt></ruby>
ise ebi

Japanese lobster

かに
kani

crab

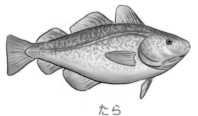

たら
tara

cod

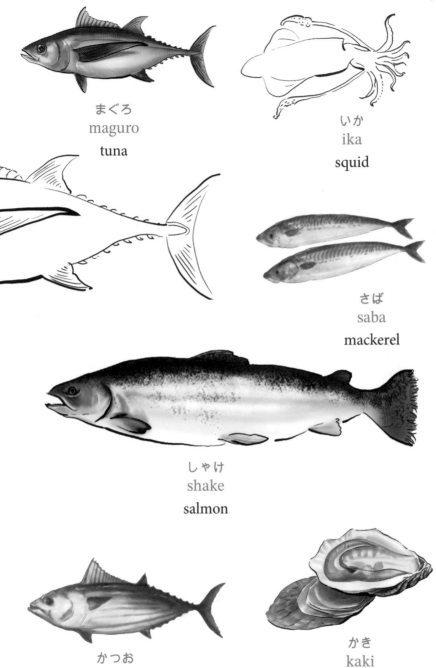

まぐろ
maguro
tuna

いか
ika
squid

さば
saba
mackerel

しゃけ
shake
salmon

かつお
katsuo
bonito

かき
kaki
oyster

<ruby>野菜<rt>やさい</rt></ruby> yasai
vegetable

In the vegetable shop

やおや
八百屋 yaoya

---

1. なす nasu
eggplant

2. きゅうり kyūri
cucumber

3. ブロッコリー burokkorī
broccoli

4. かぶ kabu
turnip

はくさい
5. 白菜 hakusai
Chinese cabbage

6. グリーンピース gurinpīsu
pea

7. カリフラワー karifurawā
cauliflower

8. にんじん ninjin
carrot

9. しそ shiso
perilla

1. しょうが shōga
ginger

---

2. レタス retasu
lettuce

---

3. かぼちゃ kabocha
pumpkin

---

4. アーモンド āmondo
almond

---

5. ピーナッツ pīnattsu
peanut

---

6. ごぼう gobō
burdok root

---

7. にんにく ninniku
garlic

---

8. きのこ kinoko
mushroom

---

9. じゃがいも jagaimo
potato

---

10. とうもろこし tōmorokoshi
corn

---

11. くるみ kurumi
walnut

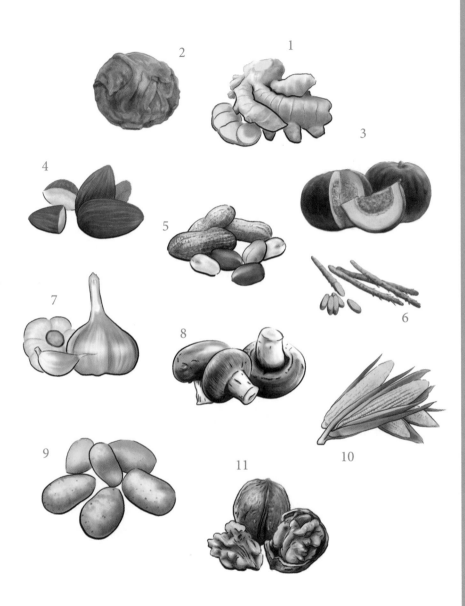

64

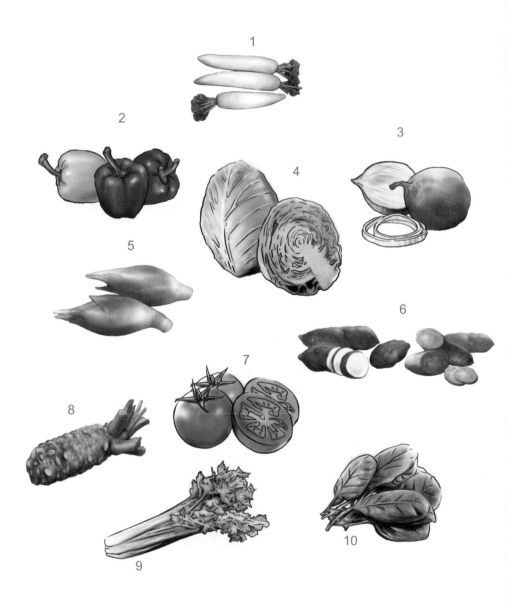

1. 大根 <ruby>だいこん</ruby> daikon
Japanese white raddish

2. ピーマン pīman
sweet pepper

3. 玉ねぎ tamanegi
onion

4. キャベツ kyabetsu
cabbage

5. みょうが myōga
Japanese ginger

6. さつまいも satsumaimo
sweet potato

7. トマト tomato
tomato

8. わさび wasabi
wasabi

9. セロリ serori
celery

10. ほうれん草 hōrensō
spinach

りんご
ringo
apple

^{あお}
青りんご
ao ringo
green apple

^{なし}
梨
nashi
pear

さくらんぼ
sakuranbo
cherry

プラム
puramu
plum

オリーブ
orību
olive

ココナッツ
kokonattsu
coconut

いちご
ichigo
strawberry

パイナップル
painappuru
pineapple

ざくろ	びわ	ラズベリー
zakuro	biwa	razuberī
pomegranate	loquat	raspberry

In the fruit shop

くだものや
果 物 屋 kudamonoya

かき 柿	ブルーベリー	ゆず
kaki	burūberī	yuzu
persimmon	blueberry	yuzu (citrus fruit)

かぼす
kabosu
kabosu(citrus fruit)

レモン
remon
lemon

アボカド
abokado
avocado

もも
桃
momo
peach

パパイヤ
papaiya
papaya

バナナ
banana
banana

マンゴー
mangō
mango

オレンジ
orenji
orange

みかん
mikan
mandarin

すいか
suika
watermelon

ぶどう
budō
grape

メロン
meron
melon

キウイ
kiui
kiwi

Beverages

の　もの
飲み物 nomimono

たんさんすい
炭酸水
tansansui
sparkling water

みず
水
mizu
water

ミネラルウォーター
mineraru wōtā
mineral water

とうにゅう
豆乳
tōnyū
soymilk

あまざけ
甘酒
amazake
sweet sake

あおじる
青汁
aojiru
green juice

にんじんジュース
ninjin jūsu
carrot juice

パイナップルジュース
painappuru jūsu
pineapple juice

りんごジュース
ringo jūsu
apple juice

トマトジュース
tomato jūsu
tomato juice

オレンジジュース
orenji jūsu
orange juice

グレープジュース
gurēpu jūsu
grape juice

At the bar

バーで　bāde

ビール
bīru
beer

にほんしゅ
日本酒
nihonshu
Japanese
rice wine

ウィスキー
wisukī
whiskey

しょうちゅう
焼酎
shōchū
Japanese
liquor

あか
赤ワイン
aka wain
red wine

しろ
白ワイン
shiro wain
white wine

ロゼワイン
roze wain
rosé wine

ゆずしゅ
柚子酒
yuzushu
yuzu wine

うめしゅ
梅酒
umeshu
plum wine

あわもり
泡盛
awamori
Okinawa
liquor

はっぽうしゅ
発泡酒
happōshu
light root beer

悪<ruby>い<rt>わる</rt></ruby>ワインを

<ruby>飲<rt>の</rt></ruby>むには、

<ruby>人生<rt>じん せい</rt></ruby>は

<ruby>余<rt>あま</rt></ruby>りにも<ruby>短<rt>みじか</rt></ruby>すぎる。

warui wain o
nomu ni wa,
jinsei wa amarinimo mijika sugiru

Life is too short to drink bad wine.

Johann Wolfgang von Goethe

エスプレッソ
esupuresso
Espresso

エスプレッソマキアート
esupuresso makiāto
Espresso
Macchiato

アメリカン
amerikān
Americano

アフォガート
afogāto
Cafe Affogato

At the coffee shop

カフェで　kafede

エスプレッソ
espresso

エスプレッソマキアート
double espresso with milk foam

アメリカン
Americano

アフォガート
espresso with ice cream

ミルクワォーム
milk foam

みず
水
water

アイスクリーム
ice cream

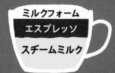

カフェラテ
kafe rate
Cafe Latte

カプチーノ
kapuchīno
Cappuccino

モカ
moka
Mocha

ホットチョコレート
hotto chokorēto
Hot chocolate

ホットミルク
hotto miruku
Hot milk

カフェラテ
milk coffee

カプチーノ
cappuccino

モカ
espresso with chocolate syrup

ホットチョコレート
hot chocolate

ホットミルク
hot milk

生クリーム
cream

スチームミルク
steamed milk

チョコレートシロツプ
chocolate syrup

1

2

4

3

5

Tea

ちゃ
お茶 ocha

6

7

8

9

10

11

12

1. <ruby>抹茶<rt>まっちゃ</rt></ruby>　matcha

matcha

2. <ruby>緑茶<rt>りょくちゃ</rt></ruby>　ryokucha

green tea

3. <ruby>昆布茶<rt>こんぶちゃ</rt></ruby>　konbucha

kelp tea

4. <ruby>桜茶<rt>さくらちゃ</rt></ruby>　sakuracha

sakura tea

5. <ruby>抹茶<rt>まっちゃ</rt></ruby>ラテ　matcha rate

matcha latte

6. <ruby>玄米茶<rt>げんまいちゃ</rt></ruby>　genmaicha

Japanese brown rice green tea

7. <ruby>福茶<rt>ふくちゃ</rt></ruby>　fukucha

fuku tea (lucky tea)

8. <ruby>蕎麦茶<rt>そばちゃ</rt></ruby>　sobacha

buckwheat tea

9. ウーロン<ruby>茶<rt>ちゃ</rt></ruby>　ūroncha

oolong tea

10. ほうじ<ruby>茶<rt>ちゃ</rt></ruby>　hōjicha

roasted green tea

11. <ruby>紅茶<rt>こうちゃ</rt></ruby>　kōcha

black tea

12. <ruby>麦茶<rt>むぎちゃ</rt></ruby>　mugicha

barley tea

In the restaurant

レストランにて resutoran nite

いらっしゃいませ！
irasshaimase
Welcome!

レストラン resutoran restaurant

メニュー menyū menu

ぜんさい
前菜 zensai starter

メインコース mein kōsu main course

デザート dezāto dessert

なんめいさま
何名様ですか。
nanmeisama desuka

How many people?

ふたり さんにん よにん
二人 / 三人 / 四人 です
futari / sannin / yonindesu

two / three / four of us

きょう なん
今日のおすすめは何ですか。
kyōno osusumewa nandesuka

What is today's special?

ねが
…をお願いします。
…o onegaishimasu

(I would like) … please.

すみません、注文をお願いします。
sumimasen, chūmono onegaishimasu
Excuse me, I would like to order, please.

この地域の名物料理は何ですか。
konochiikino meibutsu-ryoriwa nandesuka

What is the specialty of this region?

しょくじ 食事	shokuji	meals
ちょうしょく 朝食	chō shoku	breakfast
ちゅうしょく 昼食	chū shoku	lunch
ゆうしょく 夕食	yū shoku	dinner

ごゆっくり
お召し上がりください
goyukkuri omeshiagari kudasai

Enjoy your meal!

かんじょう　ねが

お勘定をお願いします。
okanjōo onegai shimasu

May I have the bill, please?

いただきます。 itadakimasu	Thank you for the food. (say before eating)
おいしい! oishii	Delicious!
とてもおいしかったです! totemo oishikattadesu	The food was very good!
ごちそうさまでした。 gochisōsamadeshita	Thank you for the food. (say after eating)

こしょう
胡椒
koshō

pepper

しお
塩
shio

salt

Seasonings

ちょうみりょう
調味料 chōmiryō

みりん
mirin

mirin

わさび
wasabi

wasabi

カレー粉
karē-ko

curry powder

しちみとうがらし
七味唐辛子
shichimi tōgarashi
chili powder

ケチャップ
ketchappu
ketchup

マヨネーズ
mayonēzu
mayonnaise

さとう
砂糖
satō
sugar

しょうゆ
醤油
shōyu
soy sauce

みそ
味噌
miso
miso

す
酢
su
vinegar

さんしょう
山椒
sanshō
sansho

84

はちみつ
hachimitsu
honey

いちごジャム
ichigo jamu
strawberry jam

ヨーグルト
yōguruto
yogurt

トースト
tōsuto
toast

フレンチトースト
furenchi tōsuto
french toast

バター
batā
butter

ゆで卵
yudetamago
soft-boiled egg

ホットケーキ
hotto kēki
pancake

スクランブルエッグ
sukuranburu eggu
scrambled eggs

洋食
yōshoku
international breakfast

Breakfast

ちょうしょく
朝食 chōshoku

たまごや
卵焼き
tamagoyaki
Japanese omelette

ちゃ
お茶
ocha
tea

や　ざかな
焼き魚
yakizakana
grilled fish

ごはん
gohan
cooked rice

みそしる
味噌汁
misoshiru
miso soup

ふくさい
副菜
fukusai
side dish

わしょく
和食
washoku
traditional Japanese breakfast

Typical Japanese dishes

典型的な和食 tenkeitekina washoku

お刺身
osashimi
sliced raw fish

天ぷら
tenpura
seafood and vegetable battered
and deep-fried, dipped in special sauce

すき焼き
sukiyaki
Japanese beef hot pot

ラーメン
rāmen
ramen noodles

蕎麦
soba
soba noodles

うな丼
unadon
a bowl of rice
topped with grilled eel

おにぎり
onigiri
rice ball with flavoured filling

<ruby>お好み焼き<rt>この や</rt></ruby>
okonomiyaki
Japanese style pizza-like dish

<ruby>焼き鳥<rt>や とり</rt></ruby>
yakitori
grilled chicken

<ruby>寿司<rt>すし</rt></ruby>
sushi
sushi

<ruby>たこ焼き<rt>や</rt></ruby>
takoyaki
ball-shaped snack with octopus

とんかつ
tonkatsu
Japanese pork cutlet

<ruby>鶏のから揚げ<rt>とり あ</rt></ruby>
tori no karaage
flour-dipped fried chicken

<ruby>牛丼<rt>ぎゅうどん</rt></ruby>
gyudon
a bowl of rice
topped with beef

しゃぶしゃぶ
shabu shabu
shabu shabu
(Japanese hot pot)

<ruby>懐<rt>かい</rt>石<rt>せき</rt></ruby>

かいせき
懐石
kaiseki
traditional multi-course meal
(Originally served before a tea ceremony)

Japanese dessert

和菓子 wagashi
^{わがし}

---

1. どら焼き dorayaki

2. まんじゅう manjū

3. 花びら餅 hana bira mochi

4. あんみつ anmitsu

5. 白玉 shiratama

6. 大福 daifuku

7. お団子 odango

8. 干菓子 higashi

9. 今川焼き imagawayaki

10. 茶菓子 chagashi

11. おしるこ oshiruko

12. 羊羹 yōkan

Places to shop

買い物をする場所 kaimonoo suru basho

department stores
デパート depāto

三越	Mitsukoshi®
高島屋	Takashimaya®
そごう	Sogo®
伊勢丹	Isetan®
松坂屋	Matsuzakaya®
大丸	Daimaru®
東急	Tokyu®
阪急	Hankyu®
西武	Seibu®

convenience stores
コンビニ konbini

ファミリーマート	Family Mart®
ローソン	Lawson®
セブンイレブン	Seven Eleven®

supermarkets
スーパー sūpā

イオン	Aeon®
イトーヨーカドー	Ito Yokado®
西友	Seiyu®

ショッピングセンター

shoppingu sentā

shopping mall

店
<ruby>みせ</ruby>

mise

shop

スーパー

sūpā

supermarket

コンビニエ

konbini

convenience store

デパート

depāto

department store

Everything your heart desires

<ruby>心<rt>こころ</rt></ruby>が<ruby>望<rt>のぞ</rt></ruby>むすべて　kokoroga nozomu subete

<ruby>化粧品店<rt>けしょうひんてん</rt></ruby>
keshōhinten
cosmetic shop

<ruby>美容院<rt>び ょう いん</rt></ruby>
biyōin
hair salon

<ruby>宝石店<rt>ほうせきてん</rt></ruby>
hōsekiten
jewelry shop

<ruby>花屋<rt>はなや</rt></ruby>
hanaya
flower shop

ブティック
butikku
fashion boutique

くつや
靴屋
kutsuya
shoe shop

みやげものや
土産物屋
miyagemonoya
souvenir shop

こっとうひんてん
骨董品店
kottōhinten
antique shop

...をお願いします。
... o onegaishimas

(I would like)... please.

1枚の シャツ
ichi mai no shatsu

a shirt.

1本の ズボン
ippon no zubon

a pair of trousers.

1足の 靴
issoku no kutsu

a pair of shoes.

1組の 靴下
hitokumi no kutsushita

a pair of socks.

2枚のブラウス
ni mai no burausu

two blouses.

3枚のジャケット
san mai no jaketto

three jackets.

4枚のスカート
yon mai no sukāto

four skirts.

5枚のコート
go mai no kōto

five coats.

それは**いくら**ですか。
sorewa **ikuradesuka**

How much does it cost?

（それは）...<ruby>円<rt>えん</rt></ruby>です。
(sorewa) ... yen desu

It costs…Yen.

（それは）とても<ruby>高<rt>たか</rt></ruby>いです。
(sorewa) totemo **takaidesu**

That is very expensive.

<ruby>割引<rt>わりびき</rt></ruby>できますか。
waribiki dekimasuka

Can you give me discount?

（それは）とても<ruby>安<rt>やす</rt></ruby>いですね。
(sorewa) totemo **yasuidesune**

That is very cheap.

<ruby>結構<rt>けっこう</rt></ruby>です、ありがとうございます。
kekkodesu, arigatō gozaimasu

No more, thanks.

この<ruby>値段<rt>ねだん</rt></ruby>は<ruby>手頃<rt>てごろ</rt></ruby>です。
kononedanwa **tegorodesu**

The price is reasonable.

<ruby>短<rt>みじか</rt></ruby>すぎます / <ruby>長<rt>なが</rt></ruby>すぎます。
mijikasugimasu / nagasugimasu

It's too short / too long.

ゆるすぎます / きつすぎます。
yurusugimasu / kitsusugimasu

It's too loose / too tight.

試着^{しちゃく}してもいいですか。

試着してもいいですか。
shichakushitemo iidesuka

May I try it on?

試着室^{しちゃくしつ}はどこですか。

試着室はどこですか。
shichakushitsuwa dokodesuka

Where is the fitting room?

セール

sēru

On sale

おおやすう
大安売り
ōyasuuri
great bargain sale

ね さ
値下げ
nesake
discount

はんがく
半額
hangaku
half price

わりびき　かかく
割引価格
waribiki kakaku
at a reduced price

か　　どくひん
お買い得品
okaidokuhin
bargain

Colors

色 iro
<small>いろ</small>

白
<small>しろ</small>
shiro

white

黒
<small>くろ</small>
kuro

black

オレンジ色
<small>いろ</small>
orenji iro

orange

茶色
<small>ちゃいろ</small>
cha iro

brown

灰色
<small>はい いろ</small>
hai iro

grey

水色
<small>みず いろ</small>
mizu iro

light blue

明るい色
あか いろ
akarui iro
light color

暗い色
くら いろ
kurai iro
dark color

赤
あか
aka
red

ピンク
pinku
pink

黄色
き いろ
ki iro
yellow

緑
みどり
midori
green

青
あお
ao
blue

紫
むらさき
murasaki
purple

Numbers

すうじ
数字 sūji

0	零 (れい)	rei / zero
1	一	ichi
2	二	ni
3	三	san
4	四	yon / shi
5	五	go
6	六	roku
7	七	nana / shichi
8	八	hachi
9	九	kyū / ku
10	十	jū
11	十一	jū ichi
12	十二	jū ni
13	十三	jū san
14	十四	jū yon / jū shi
15	十五	jū go
16	十六	jū roku
17	十七	jū nana / jū shichi
18	十八	jū hachi
19	十九	jū kyū / jū ku
20	二十	nijū
21	二十一	nijū ichi
22	二十二	nijū ni
23	二十三	nijū san
24	二十四	nijū yon / nijū shi
25	二十五	nijū go
26	二十六	nijū roku
27	二十七	nijū nana/nijū shichi
28	二十八	nijū hachi

29	二十九	nijū kyū / nijū ku
30	三十	san jū
40	四十	yon jū /shi jū
50	五十	go jū
60	六十	roku jū
70	七十	nana jū / shichi jū
80	八十	hachi jū
90	九十	kyū jū
100	百	hyaku
101	百一	hyaku ichi
102	百二	hyaku ni
200	二百	ni hyaku
300	三百	san byaku
400	四百	yon hyaku
500	五百	go hyaku
600	六百	roppyaku
700	七百	nana hyaku
800	八百	happyaku
900	九百	kyū hyaku
1000	千	sen
10 000	一万	ichi man
100 000	十万	jū man
1 000 000	百万	hyaku man

1

いち ばん
一番
ichiban
first

2

に ばん
二番
niban
second

3

さん ばん
三番
samban
third

fourth	四番	yon ban
fifth	五番	go ban
sixth	六番	roku ban
seventh	七番	nana ban
eighth	八番	hachi ban
ninth	九番	kyū ban
tenth	十番	jū ban

When then?

いつ？ itsu

きのう
昨日
kinō

yesterday

きのう　よる　　　　さくばん
昨日の夜　／　昨晩
kinōnoyoru ／ sakuban

yesterday evening

おととい
一昨日
ototoi

the day before yesterday

せんしゅう
先週
senshū

last week

きょねん　さくねん
去年 ／ 昨年
kyonen ／ sakunen

last year

きょう
今日
kyō

today

あした / あす
明日
ashita/asu

tomorrow

あさって
明後日
asatte

the day after tomorrow

らいしゅう
来週
raishū

next week

らいねん
来年
rainen

next year

All about time

じかん
時間について
jikannitsuite

じかん 時間 jikan	time
とけい 時計 tokei	clock
びょう 秒 byō	second(s)
ふん / ぶん 分 fun/pun	minute(s)
ふん 15分 jūgo fun	quarter of an hour
ぶん　はん 30分 / 半 san juppun / han	half an hour
じ ~ 時 ~ ji	~ o'clock
じかん ~ 時間 ~ jikan	~ hour(s) (period of time)

午前
ごぜん
gozen
morning

正午
しょうご
shōgo
noon

午後
ごご
gogo
afternoon

夕方
ゆうがた
yūgata
evening

夜
よる
yoru
night

夜中
よなか
yonaka
middle of the night

深夜
しんや
shinya
late at night

早い
はや
hayai
early

遅い
おそ
osoi
late

<ruby>今<rt>いま</rt></ruby><ruby>何時<rt>なんじ</rt></ruby>ですか。

ima nanji desuka

What time is it?

（<ruby>午前<rt>ごぜん</rt></ruby>）7<ruby>時<rt>じ</rt></ruby>10<ruby>分<rt>ぶん</rt></ruby>です。

(gozen) shichi ji juppun desu

It's ten past seven.

（午前）1 時です。
(gozen) ichi ji desu
It's one a.m.

（午前）7 時15分です。
(gozen) shichi ji jū go fun desu
It's a quarter past seven.

（午前）8 時です。
(gozen) hachi ji desu
It's eight in the morning.

（午前）10時10分前です。
(gozen) jū ji juppun maedesu
It's ten to ten.

（午前）10時です。
(gozen) jū ji desu
It's ten in the morning.

（午前）10時10分です。
(gozen) jū ji juppun desu
It's ten past ten.

（午前）10時半です。
(gozen) jū ji han desu
It's half past ten.

<ruby>昼<rt>ひる</rt></ruby>の12時です。
hiruno jūni ji desu
It's midday.

（<ruby>午後<rt>ごご</rt></ruby>）8<ruby>時<rt>じ</rt></ruby>5<ruby>分前<rt>ふんまえ</rt></ruby>です。
(gogo) hachi ji go fun maedesu
It's five to eight in the evening

（<ruby>午後<rt>ごご</rt></ruby>）10<ruby>時<rt>じ</rt></ruby>です。
(gogo) jū ji desu
It's ten o'clock at night.

<ruby>夜<rt>よる</rt></ruby>の12時です。
yoruno jūni ji desu
It's midnight.

Seven days of the week
ようび
曜日
yōbi

げつようび 月曜日 getsuyōbi	かようび 火曜日 kayōbi	すいようび 水曜日 suiyōbi
Monday	Tuesday	Wednesday

へいじつ
平日
heijitsu — work day

しゅうまつ
週末
shūmatsu — weekend

さいじつ
祭日
saijitsu — holiday

きゅうじつ
休日
kyūjitsu — day off

もくようび 木曜日 mokuyōbi	きんようび 金曜日 kinyōbi	どようび 土曜日 doyōbi	にちようび 日曜日 nichiyōbi
Thursday	Friday	Saturday	Sunday

きょう　なんようび
今日は何曜日ですか。　　　　　　What day is it today?
kyōwa nanyōbi desuka

げつようび
月曜日です。　　　　　　　　　　It's Monday.
getsuyōbi desu

きょう　なんにち
今日は何日ですか。　　　　　　　What is today's date?
kyōwa nannichi desuka

がつ　か
1月10日です。　　　　　　　　　It's the 10th of January.
ichi gatsu tōka desu

きょう　やす
今日はお休みですか。　　　　　　Is today a holiday?
kyōwa oyasumi desuka

1
いちがつ
一月
ichi gatsu
January

2
に がつ
二月
ni gatsu
February

5
ご がつ
五月
go gatsu
May

6
ろく がつ
六月
roku gatsu
June

9
く がつ
九月
ku gatsu
September

10
じゅう がつ
十月
jū gatsu
October

The twelve months of the year

12 ヶ月　jūni kagetsu
<small>かげつ</small>

3

さんがつ
三月
san gatsu
March

4

しがつ
四月
shi gatsu
April

7

しちがつ
七月
shichi gatsu
July

8

はちがつ
八月
hachi gatsu
August

11

じゅういちがつ
十一月
jūichi gatsu
November

12

じゅうにがつ
十二月
jūni gatsu
December

The weather and seasons

天気と季節 tenkito kisetsu

春
haru
spring

夏
natsu
summer

秋
aki
autumn

冬
fuyu
winter

今日の天気はどうですか。
kyōno tenkiwa dōdesuka

What's the weather like today?

今日は天気がいいです。
kyōwa tenkiga iidesu

The weather is fine today.

晴れです。
hare desu

It's sunny.

今日は天気が悪いです。
kyōwa tenkiga waruidesu

The weather is bad today.

暑いです。
atsuidesu

It's hot.

とても暑いです。
totemo atsuidesu

It's very hot.

蒸し暑いです。
mushiatsuidesu

It's muggy.

寒いです。
samuidesu

It's cold.

とても寒いです。
totemo samuidesu

I'm freezing.

風が強いです。
kazega tsuyoidesu

It's windy.

霧です。
kiri desu

It's foggy.

雨です。
ame desu

It's rainy.

霧雨です。
kirisame desu

It's drizzling.

雪が降っています。
yukiga futteimasu

It's snowing.

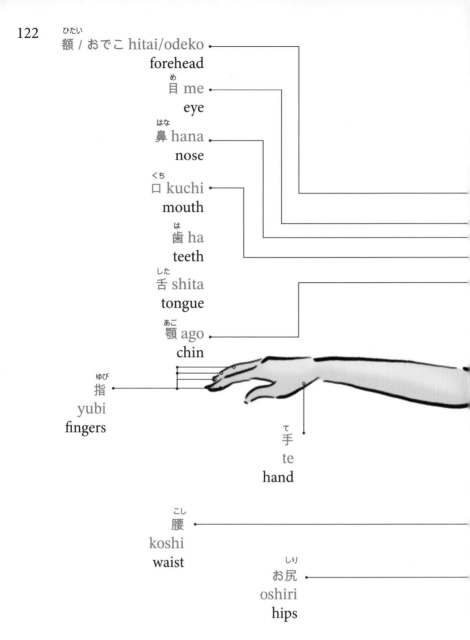

ひたい
額 / おでこ hitai/odeko
forehead

め
目 me
eye

はな
鼻 hana
nose

くち
口 kuchi
mouth

は
歯 ha
teeth

した
舌 shita
tongue

あご
顎 ago
chin

ゆび
指
yubi
fingers

て
手
te
hand

こし
腰
koshi
waist

しり
お尻
oshiri
hips

Parts of the body

からだ ぶ い
体の部位 karadano bui

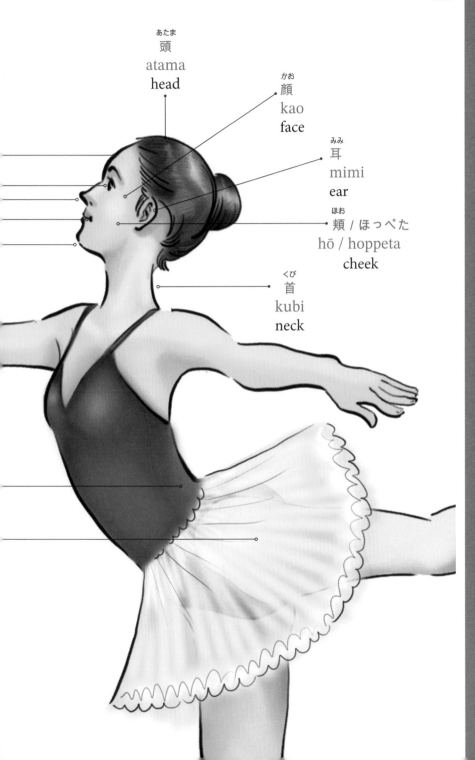

あたま
頭
atama
head

かお
顔
kao
face

みみ
耳
mimi
ear

ほお
頬 / ほっぺた
hō / hoppeta
cheek

くび
首
kubi
neck

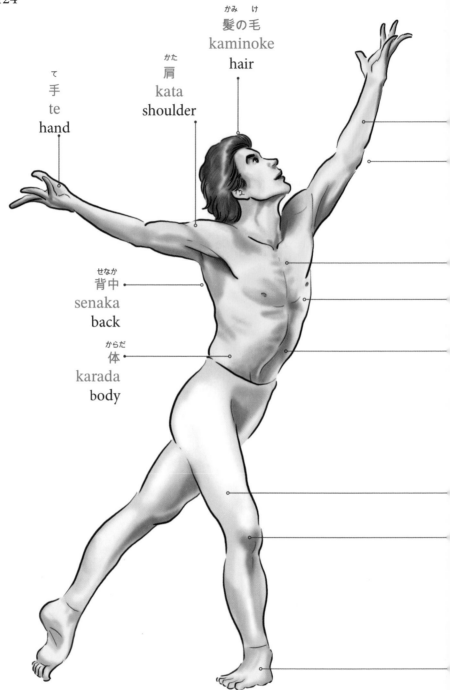

<ruby>髪<rt>かみ</rt></ruby>の<ruby>毛<rt>け</rt></ruby>
kaminoke
hair

<ruby>肩<rt>かた</rt></ruby>
kata
shoulder

<ruby>手<rt>て</rt></ruby>
te
hand

<ruby>背中<rt>せなか</rt></ruby>
senaka
back

<ruby>体<rt>からだ</rt></ruby>
karada
body

うで
腕
ude
arm

ひじ
肘
hiji
elbow

むね
胸
mune
chest

しんぞう
心臓
shinzō
heart

なか
お腹
onaka
stomach

あし
脚
ashi
leg

ひざ
膝
hiza
knee

あし
足
ashi
foot

Everyday activities

<ruby>日常<rt>にちじょう</rt></ruby><ruby>生活<rt>せいかつ</rt></ruby> nichijyō seikatsu

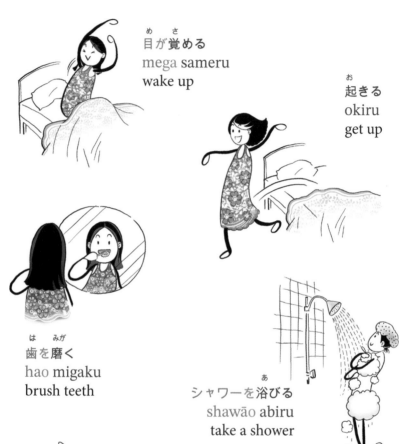

目が<ruby>覚<rt>さ</rt></ruby>める
mega sameru
wake up

起きる
okiru
get up

歯を<ruby>磨<rt>みが</rt></ruby>く
hao migaku
brush teeth

シャワーを<ruby>浴<rt>あ</rt></ruby>びる
shawāo abiru
take a shower

お<ruby>風呂<rt>ふろ</rt></ruby>に<ruby>入<rt>はい</rt></ruby>る
ofuroni hairu
take a bath

りょうり
料理する
ryōrisuru
cook

た
食べる
taberu
eat

の
飲む
nomu
drink

か
書く
kaku
write

よ
読む
yomu
read

み
見る
miru
look at

<ruby>待<rt>ま</rt></ruby>つ
matsu
wait

<ruby>会<rt>あ</rt></ruby>う
au
meet

あげる
ageru
give

<ruby>喜<rt>よろこ</rt></ruby>ぶ
yorokobu
be glad

<ruby>踊<rt>おど</rt></ruby>る
odoru
dance

<ruby>笑<rt>わら</rt></ruby>う
warau
laugh/smile

<ruby>泣<rt>な</rt></ruby>く
naku
cry

<ruby>去<rt>さ</rt></ruby>る
saru
leave

<ruby>電話<rt>でんわ</rt></ruby>する
denwasuru
call on the telephone

スポーツを**する**
supōtsuo suru
do sports

<ruby>観察<rt>かんさつ</rt></ruby>する
kansatsusuru
watch

<ruby>絵<rt>え</rt></ruby>を<ruby>描<rt>か</rt></ruby>く
eo kaku
paint

うた
歌う
utau
sing

しゃしん　と
写真を撮る
shashino toru
take pictures

たの
楽しむ
tanoshimu
have fun

う
売る
uru
sell

か
買う
kau
buy

はたら
働く
hataraku
work

なら
習う
narau
learn

おし
教える
oshieru
teach

だ
抱きしめる
dakishimeru
hug

あい
愛する
aisuru
love

キスする
kisusuru
kiss

けっこん
結婚する
kekkonsuru
marry

When you feel sick

きぶん わる
気分が悪くなったとき
kibunga warukunattatoki

きぶん わる 気分が悪いです。 kibunga waruidesu	I don't feel well.
は け 吐き気がします。 hakikega shimasu	I feel like I'm going to vomit.
むかむかします。 mukamuka shimasu	I feel nauseous.
いた ここが痛いです。 kokoga itaidesu	It hurts here.
ねつ 熱があります。 netsuga arimasu	I have a fever.
ずつう 頭痛がします。 zutsūga shimasu	I have a headache.
なか いた お腹が痛いです。 onakaga itaidesu	I have a stomachache.

喉<ruby>のど</ruby>が**痛**<ruby>いた</ruby>いです。
nodoga itaidesu

I have a sore throat.

腰痛<ruby>ようつう</ruby>があります。
yōtsūga arimasu

I have backache.

歯<ruby>は</ruby>が**痛**<ruby>いた</ruby>いです。
haga itaidesu

I have a toothache.

便秘<ruby>べんぴ</ruby>です。
benpi desu

I am constipated.

下痢<ruby>げり</ruby>です。
geri desu

I have diarrhea.

アレルギーがあります。
arerugīga arimasu

I have an allergy.

発疹<ruby>ほっしん</ruby>がでました。
hosshinga demashita

I have a rash.

やっきょく
薬局
yakkyoku
pharmacy

びょう いん
病院 byōin
hospital

くすり
薬 kusuri
medicine

い しゃ
医者 isha
doctor

は い しゃ
歯医者 haisha
dentist

かん ご し
看護師 kangoshi
nurse

かんじゃ
患者 kanjya
patient

きゅう きゅうしゃ
救急車 kyūkyūsha
ambulance

だいじ
お大事に！
odaijini

Bless you!

Urgency

きんきゅうじたい
緊急事態 kinkyū jitai

トイレはどこですか。
toirewa dokodesuka

Where is the restroom?

わたし　　　　　　　　　い
（私は）トイレに行きたいです。
(watashiwa) toireni ikitaidesu

I need to use the restroom.

この<ruby>近<rt>ちか</rt></ruby>くにトイレはありますか。
konochikakuni toirewa arimasuka

Is there a public restroom near here?

（私は）病院に行きたいです。
(watashiwa) byōinni ikitaidesu

I need to go to the hospital.

助けて!　警察を呼んでください!
tasukete　keisatsuo yonde kudasai

Help!　Call the police, please!

What do these signs mean?

ひょうしき　いみ　なん
標識の意味は何でしょう？
hyōshikinoimiwa nandeshō

と
止まれ
tomare
STOP

しゃりょうしんにゅうきんし
車両進入禁止
sharyō shinnyū kinshi
NO ENTRY

ほこうしゃつうこうど
歩行者通行止め
hokōsha tsūkōdome
NO PEDESTRIANS

じょこう
徐行
jokō
SLOW DOWN

どそくげんきん
土足厳禁
dosoku genkin
SHOES STRICTLY
PROHIBITED

コインロッカー
koin rokkā
COIN LOCKER

いっぽうつうこう
一方通行
ippō tsukō
ONE WAY

ちゅうしゃじょう
駐車場
chūshajō
PARKING

ちゅうていしゃきんし
駐停車禁止
chūteisha kinshi
PARKING AND STOPPING
PROHIBITED

ちゅうしゃきんし
駐車禁止
chūsha kinshi
NO PARKING

おうだんほどう
横断歩道
ōdan hodō
PEDESTRIAN CROSSING

ほこうしゃ せんよう どうろ
歩行者専用道路
hokōsha senyō dōro
PEDESTRIAN ROAD

つうがくろ
通学路
tsūgakuro

SCHOOL ZONE

ひなんばしょ
避難場所
hinan basho

EVACUATION SITE

の　　　ば
タクシー乗り場
takushī noriba

TAXI STAND

の　　ば
バス乗り場
basu noriba

BUS STOP

でんしゃの　　ば
電車乗り場
densha noriba

TRAIN STATION

エスカレーター
esukarētā

ESCALATOR

トイレ
toire

TOILET

おんすいせんじょうべんざ
温水洗浄便座
onsui senjō benza

BIDET

ようしき
洋式トイレ
yōshiki toire

TOILET
(WESTERN STYLE)

わしき
和式トイレ
washiki toire

TOILET
(JAPANESE STYLE)

つなみひなんばしょ
津波避難場所
tsunami hinan basho

TSUNAMI SHELTER

おんせん
温泉
onsen

HOT SPRING

Emotional outbursts

In this chapter we will be dealing with something rather special: emotional outbursts. What, you may ask, does this have to do with a book aimed at introducing a foreign language?

I know that this is quite a sensitive issue and I'm pretty sure that you don't know any other language books that deal with the topic. As I say, I'm inviting you on a risky adventure. But I think it's absolutely essential for you and really useful. I think you need to know this because it can help you to avoid very embarrassing situations when you are in Japan.

First, let me explain what I mean by emotional outbursts. What exactly are they? They are words that simply tumble out of your mouth. You don't usually give them a second thought – they just pop out – and can't be popped back in again, once they're out.

When we are angry, disappointed, afraid, surprised or delighted, we use emotional outbursts to let off steam and regain our calm. We can think of them as turbulence tranquilizers for our emotions.

These outbursts can be more or less violent, depending on intonation and the particular intention or situation in which they are spoken. Gentle outbursts can be mumbled to ourselves to cool our spirits. Violent emotional outbursts are often insulting and deeply hurtful. This type is known in Japanese as 罵倒語 (batōgo)

So, you can probably now appreciate how difficult and tricky this whole topic is. The fact that I bring up this topic may be unpleasant for the Japaneses who are often reserved and polite by nature. However, my intentions are entirely good. I don't want to insult or ridicule their language, but simply to help you avoid making a fool of yourself.

If you hear these Japanese words and try to copy them, it's more than likely that you'll get the exact intonation wrong, or it won't come out at quite the right moment, or be appropriate for the person or situation you're in.

So, my first tip is: don't block your ears when you hear them, but don't just copy them either. As a foreigner, you need to get to know them but use them carefully, and only if you're absolutely certain about how and when.

But even if you never use these outbursts yourself, it is certainly helpful to know them. It might avoid a few embarrassing situations or even a slap around the face. This is one of the main reasons for dealing with these phrases.

I hope I've been able to make clear why this topic is an important one in language learning.

Now let's get started:

The first word we will be looking at is the word くそ! (kuso)

Don't worry – your own language almost certainly has an equivalent expression. What's more, the literal meaning is really quite banal and describes the organic waste product from our digestive system. That's not really so bad, is it?

Of course, it's not this literal meaning that is intended when this word is used as an emotional outburst. What the expression means in this case is that the present situation or circumstance is so unpleasant and disgusting as the direct contact with the digestive waste.

Here's a classic example of such a situation: you desperately need to relieve yourself but the only toilet you find is occupied. You can't hold back much longer and in desperation you shout out くそ! (kuso) ("Shit!").

With a bit of luck the current occupant will take note of your desperation and vacate the WC in time.

Another common outburst which is not quite as strong is the word 最悪! (saiaku) (literally "worst"). This expression will give you the opportunity to let off steam, and calm down, the same way as "Oh, shit!" in English does.

Now come the three Japanese emotinal outbursts which have approximately the same meaning:

バカ! (baka) 、アホ! (aho) 、ボケ! (boke)

All three are used in the similar situations. They are translated as: stupit, idiot, and brainless respectively.

The following two expressions convey similar meaning as English emotinal outburst: Shut up!

They are うるせー! (uruse) Literal meaning is "noisy or annoying ", and だまれ! (damare) Literal meaning is "stop talking".

The next set of emotinal outburst is このやろう (konoyarō) and ばかやろう! (bakayarō). These two words are rather harsh. Either expression will give you the opportunity to speak your mind or communicate your opinions, the same way as "You fool!" or "You idiot!" in English does.

And these two words also have strong negative meaning. It's used to express our wish that the person we are talking to should go to hell immediately: 死ね! (shine) and くたばれ! (kutabare)

Finally, dear readers, let me assure you that I have tried to do all I can to deal with such a sensitive and controversial issue without embarrassing you. I strongly believe that it is important to give you as much confidence as possible when starting to learn the Japanese language.

Knowing something about how people express their feelings and emotions is part of that process. I could continue on this theme for some time, but it's enough for you to have a clear idea of the topic, so that you can avoid any embarrassing situations.

Never forget that emotional outburst can vary in meaning as well as in intensity. If you hear one of these phrases, see if you can hear whether the speaker is angry, dissatisfied, furious, or perhaps cracking a joke or making fun of someone.

As far as possible, avoid using these outbursts yourself. Remember, that these words have the power to insult and hurt others and can also be dangerous for you. By using them you are likely to put yourself in a very embarrassing situation, and quite possibly lose face in the process.

きれい!
kirei
Beautiful!

すごい!
sugoi
Brilliant!

さいこう
最高!
saikō
The best!

かんぺき
完璧!
kanpeki
Perfect!

Compliments

褒め言葉 homekotoba

素晴らしい!
subarashii
Wonderful!

素敵!
suteki
Lovely!

Romance

ロマンス romansu

とても**かっこいいです**ね。
totemo kakkoiidesune
You are so handsome.

きれいな目をしていますね。
kireinameo shiteimasune
You have beautiful eyes.

やさしいですね。
yasashiidesune
You are so kind.

恋人はいますか。
koibitowa imasuka
Do you have boyfriend/girlfriend?

大好きです。
daisukidesu
I like you very much.

愛しています。
aishiteimasu
I love you.

とてもかわいいですね。

totemokawaiidesune

You are so cute.

すてき
素敵ですね。
sutekidesune

You are lovely.

<ruby>愛<rt>あい</rt></ruby>しています。
aishiteimasu

I love you.

<ruby>結婚<rt>けっこん</rt></ruby>してくれますか。

kekkonshite kuremasuka

Will you marry me?

<ruby>魅力的<rt>みりょくてき</rt></ruby>です。
miryokutekidesu

You are gorgeous.

Land and people

ちいき　　ひとびと
地域と人々
chiiki to hitobito

RUSSiA

NORTH
KOREA

SOUTH
KOREA

Sea of Japan

北海道
Hokkaido

青森
Aomori

秋田
Akita

岩手
Iwate

福島
Fukushima

NORTH
PACIFIC
OCEAN

京都
Kyoto

長野
Nagano

埼玉
Saitama

岐阜
Gifu

愛知
Aichi

東京
Tokyo

千葉
Chiba

広島
Hiroshima

福岡
Fukuoka

愛媛
Ehime

奈良
Nara

静岡
Shizuoka

神奈川
Kanagawa

長崎
Nagasaki

高知
Kochi

大阪
Osaka

山梨
Yamanashi

沖縄
Okinawa

鹿児島
Kagoshima

If you want to learn about the shape and form of Japan, the simplest thing to do is to look at a map. If you want to know more about the people, how they think, how they lead their lives, then the best method is to look at their proverbs. They reveal how the Japanese think.

Often proverbs have developed over centuries as the result of local people's experiences and of the way they think and live their lives. These sayings are passed on from one generation to the next, together with the emotions and moods they convey. Here are a few memorable Japanese proverbs:

七転び八起き。
nanakorobi yaoki
Fall down seven times, get up eight.

思い立ったが吉日。
omoitattaga kichijitsu
Strike while the iron is hot.

失敗は成功のもと。
shippaiwa seikonomoto
Every failure is a stepping stone to success.

継続は力なり。
keizokuwa chikaranari
Perseverance makes you stronger.

笑う門には福来る。
waraukadoniwa fukukitaru
Good fortune and happiness come to the homes of those who smile.

Now you will be able to savor the Japanese language like a delicatessen. Any worries you may have had about learning this language will turn to joyful confidence.

Japanese
at your Fingertips

by
Tien Tammada

Original title: พูดญี่ปุ่นซะหน่อย เทียร ธรรมดา
© Leelaaphasa Co., Ltd.
63/120 Moo 8, Tambon Saothonghin, Bangyai District,
Nonthaburi 11140 Thailand
E-Mail: leelaaphasa2008@gmail.com
All rights reserved.

1. Edition 2023 (1,01 - 2023)
© PONS Langenscheidt GmbH, Stöckachstraße 11, 70190 Stuttgart, 2023

Translation: Ta Tammadien, David Thorn
Proofreader: Yoko Baba, Klangjai Patanant
Cover Design: Sira Illner, Leonie Eul
Illustration Inside: K. Kiattisak, Purmpoon Khamnuanta
Photo Credit Cover: Kyoto: Shutterstock, Canicula; japanese flag:
Shutterstock, chekart; cherry blossom branch: Shutterstock, Alexander_P;
motorcycle: Shutterstock, Net Vector
Typesetting/Layout: Wachana Leuwattananon, Ta Tammadien
Printing: Multiprint GmbH, Konstinbrod

ISBN 978-3-12-514553-5